MOOD

… prese

MW00531723

Joyful

This edition published by Parragon Books Ltd in 2017
and distributed by

Parragon Inc
440 Park Avenue South, 13th Floor
New York, NY 10016
www.parragon.com

Copyright © Parragon Books Ltd 2017

Written and illustrated by Emily Portnoi

ISBN 978-1-4748-4184-9

Printed in China

MOODLES

··· presents ···

Joyful

PaRRagon

Bath · New York · Cologne · Melbourne · Delhi
Hong Kong · Shenzhen · Singapore

WELCOME
to your moodle book.

"What is a moodle?" I hear you ask.
Well, a moodle is just a doodle with the power
to change your mood. Be it grumpy to glad, awful
to joyful, or glad back to mad. Cheaper than therapy,
quicker than chanting chakras, tastier than a cabbage
leaf and sandpaper detox, and less fattening than
chocolate cake!

The moodle: a simple thing that
can really turn your day around.

All you need is a pen or pencil, imagination, and an open mind. Be prepared to delve into your innermost thoughts, ideas, and concepts. Uncover your subconscious and lay it bare on the page — admire it, mock it, and marvel at it until you feel altogether much chirpier. Let the moodle wisdom penetrate your subconscious and guide you on a magical mental journey, following the mark you make, until the final stop — joy!

Sketch your *good intention* for the day.

Moodle a spring in your step.

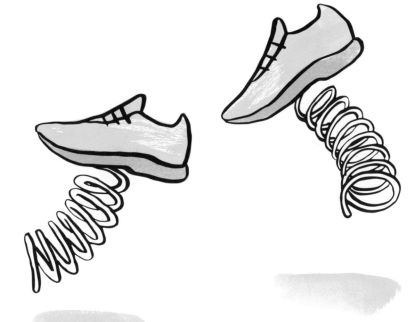

Give these bees
something to **BUZZ** about.

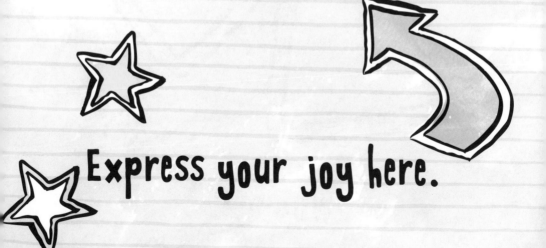

Express your joy here.

Who brings you joy?

Have patience ...

Come back to this page last.

Find your inner joy.

Moodle your glass half FULL of cheer.

SWEET DREAMS...

Sketch the scene you'd most like to dream.

Catch the best dream you've ever had.

Moodle your joys of spring.

JUMP IN PUDDLES.

Moodle your gorgeously squelchy puddle.

KICK THE LEAVES.

Moodle your crisp, golden, fall leaves.

YOUR SHIP IS FINALLY COMING IN!

DRAW WHAT YOU'D LIKE TO SEE ON BOARD.

Embrace this moment.

Draw what you can see right now.

Moodle blossom onto this tree.

Moodle your path to ...

A SMILE is contagious.

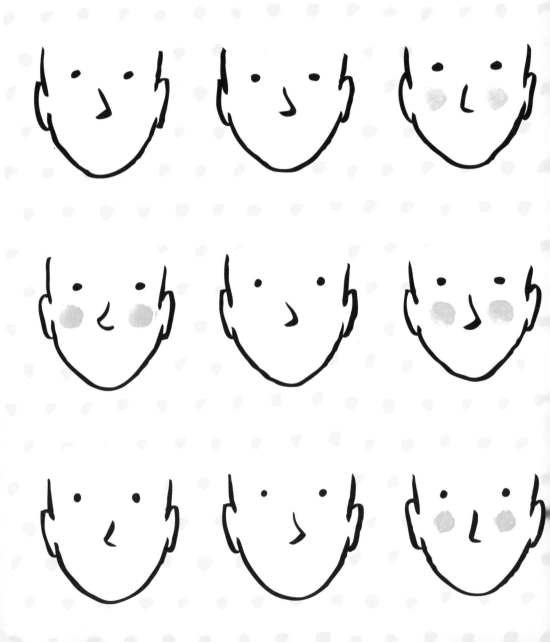

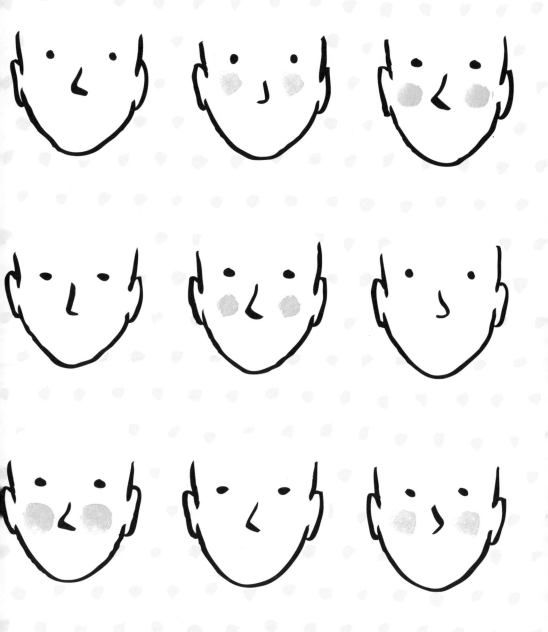

Sketch a smiley face a day.

TAKE A LEAP INTO THE UNKNOWN.

Moodle something you've never moodled before.

FREE your guilty pleasures.

Don't forget to lift your head every once in a while.

Moodle what you see directly above you right now.

GIVING IS JOYFUL.

Draw a picture, tear it out, and give it to someone.

Moodle a mate for this lonely lobster.

Be your own cheerleader ...

...write a PEPPY chant, then repeat it daily.

Moodle yourself at the TOP of the pyramid.

Moodle to music ...

 ...classical.

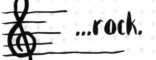 ...rock.

...jazz.

- -

...reggae.

A Joy to behold.

Moodle your favorite sight.

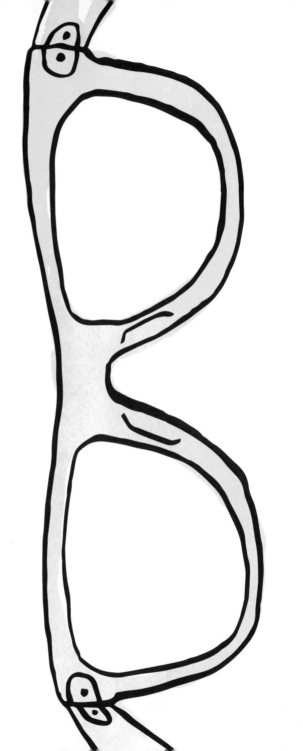

Today is a GOOD-NEWS DAY.
Moodle your cover story.

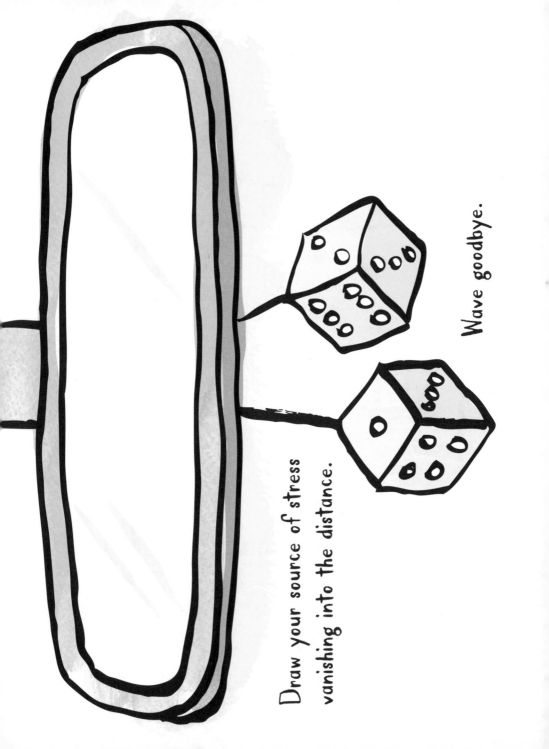

Draw your source of stress vanishing into the distance.

Wave goodbye.

DO A JOYFUL DANCE.

Moodle the top half of yourself here.
Cut out the two circles, pop your fingers through, and cut loose.

Draw yourself crossing the
FINISH LINE.

Moodle on the sunny side.

Don't be UNDER the weather.

Moodle yourself above the clouds.

Draw a beautiful horizon,

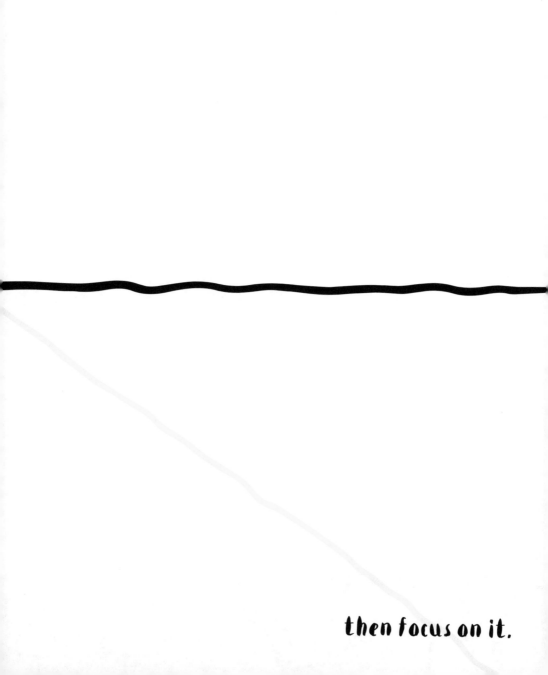

then focus on it.

Moodle yourself as a bird soaring high.

WANTED

★

MY JOY

Description:

Last seen:

Draw the way you did on your FIRST DAY OF SCHOOL!

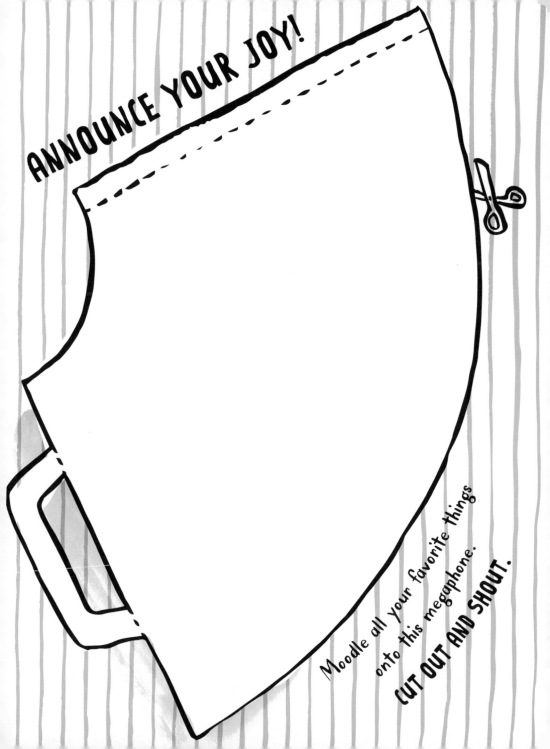

ANNOUNCE YOUR JOY!

Moodle all your favorite things onto this megaphone. **CUT OUT AND SHOUT.**

HOW TO MAKE YOUR MEGAPHONE

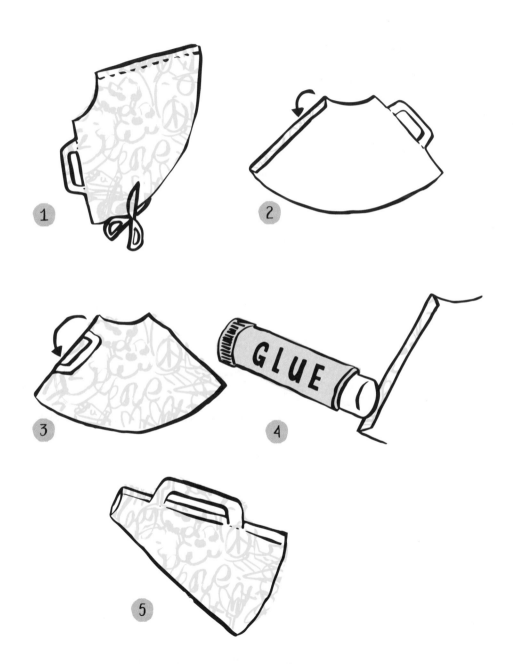

Moodle what you'd like to find at
the end of the rainbow.

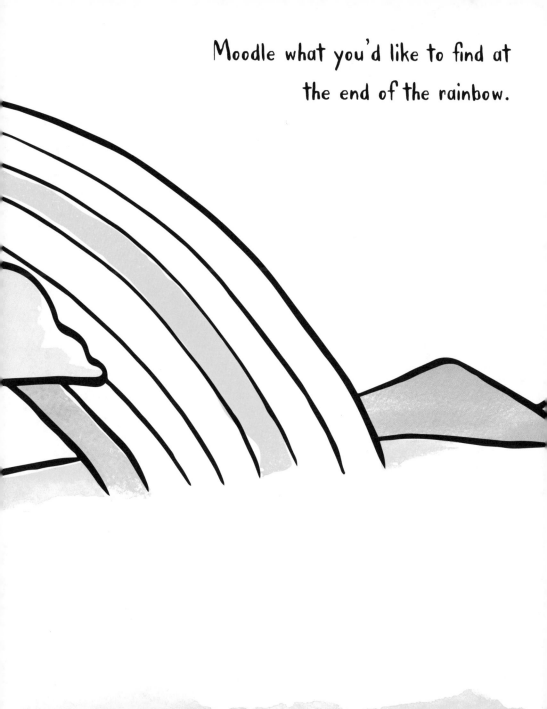

Invite joy to your party.

Moodle an invitation here.

Color your cupcake.

Fill your head entirely with **JOYFUL MOODLES,**

so there's just no room for negative thoughts to creep in.

MOODLE YOURSELF ON TOP OF THE WORLD.

Send joy, to receive joy...

Moodle five positive things you'd like to happen to other people in your life.

Moodle five positive things you'd like to happen in *your* life.

Write a thank-you letter
to your joy. List everything
you are grateful for.

Moodle FIVE WAYS in which you are a BETTER, STRONGER, or more ENLIGHTENED person today than you were this time last year.

What would go into your ULTIMATE juice?

Draw your favorite compliment.

Then tear this page out and fix it on your mirror.

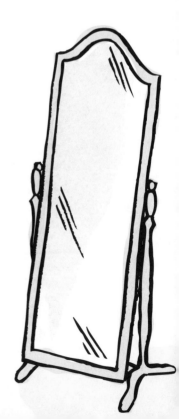

FIND JOY IN YOUR FAMILY AND FRIENDS' SUCCESSES.

MOODLE THEM ONTO THIS TROPHY.

Give a BIG SHOUT-OUT
to everyone you love.

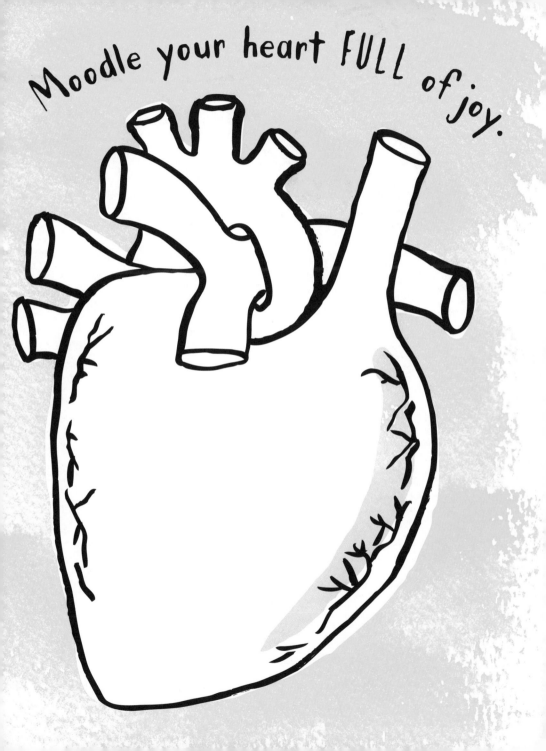

WHAT'S YOUR **SECRET** TO LIFE?

We are shaped
by our thoughts.

Moodle five positive
thoughts here.

Moodle your hand here,
then give yourself a BIG HIGH FIVE.

Revel in the joy of art.

Moodle like nobody is watching.

Moodle your seeds of joy—
watch them grow.

Draw your GREATEST achievement.

Moodle a pal for this magpie
and turn sorrow into joy.

Joy needs space to grow.

Keep growing this moodle to the
edge of the page and beyond.

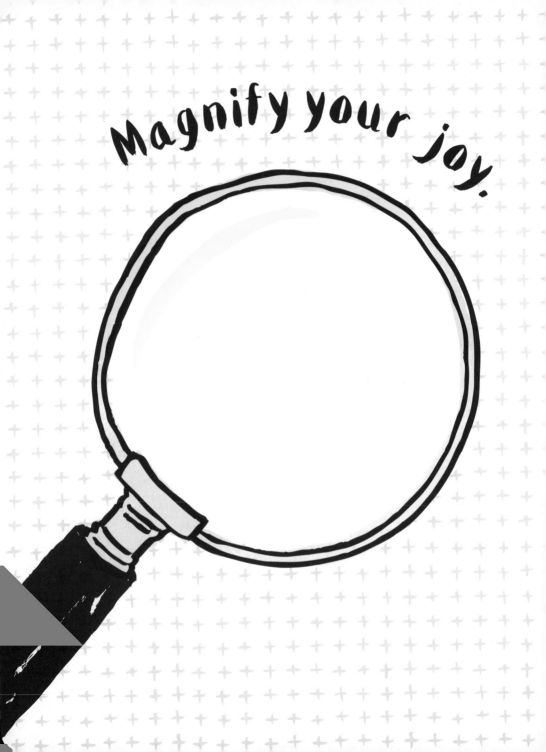

REACH FOR THE STARS.

QUICK-FIRE MOODLES.

Draw the first thing you think
of when you read ...

BLISS

SPECIAL

SING

Take pleasure in the little things.

Moodle four fabulous things that could fit inside a matchbox.

FILL THIS PAGE WITH KISSES.

Moodle what floats your boat.

Give these shapes a smiley face and moodle yourself five new friends.

LOOSEN UP. Try again, but go over the lines this time.

COUNT YOUR BLESSINGS.

Sketch them onto these counters.

Moodle a sunrise.

DRAW YOUR WORST HABIT HERE.

RIP OUT THE PAGE, THROW IT AWAY,
CURE YOURSELF OF THAT BAD HABIT FOREVER.

DON'T LET YOURSELF GET TIED UP IN KNOTS.

Follow the path to the other side.

Beginning

End

Love yourself.

Moodle your FAVORITE character trait.

Moodle your FAVORITE feature.

Then stop and admire.

Take control of your destiny.

Moodle five wishes for your future onto these fortune cookies.

Try not to eat them.

Moodle your guardian angel.

ell a story with moodles.

PRIORITIZE YOURSELF!
Draw a self-portrait here.

Celebrate the BEST things in your life.

Give them each an award for being AWESOME.

Let go of the things in your life that DON'T WORK.

Draw them here, then tear out the page and TOSS IT AWAY.

good riddance!

SHARE THE JOY!

Find a friend and moodle together.

LET THE SUN SHINE!
Moodle your ultimate seven-day forecast.

MONDAY

TUESDAY

WEDNESDAY

THURSDAY

FRIDAY

SATURDAY

SUNDAY

Fill this album page with your most
JOYFUL MEMORIES.

All moodles complete and wisdom absorbed, you will by now have reached a state of complete euphoric joyfulness. Perhaps you are even floating on a higher mental plane, radiating love, light, and positivity.

Next time you need a little joyful lift, simply revisit the pages of this book to put the spring back in your step.